INTRODUCTION

The Beach Boys' music has served as a great companion throughout our lives with songs that highlighted our happiest days and provided us the most compassionate shoulder to cry on. Breaking creative boundaries at every turn, they have proven to be a band for all seasons. Yet what was able to set The Beach Boys apart from the pack was their ability to inspire. This music captured our imaginations and acted as the springboard to new and exciting experiences. These sounds remain joyful, spiritual, and fully in the now.

Never underestimate the power and promise of COOL. Beach Boys music keeps you engaged, it keeps you moving, and urges you to stay young.

The imagery contained in The Beach Boys' catalogue spans far beyond the sun and fun of the early hits and drag race anthems. This group dove deep into the ways of the heart with passionate love, ecological pursuits, the wide open sea and plains, the old west, spiritual enlightenment, and even the solar system.

The Beach Boys are all that and so much more.

What's so special about THIS book is that it works on so many levels. If you simply love coloring, or drawing, or graphics – it's all there. For the die-hard Beach Boys fan, the attention to detail and history peppered throughout the pages is a gentle nod reminding you you're not alone. There are in-jokes and insider references throughout.

While looking at this book for the first time, I was captivated. As both an artist and lifelong Beach Boys fan, I've never seen s_____ this – and never imagined I would. St_____ te a project that check_____ it thrills, and it mov

The Beach Boys have spent their lives sharing their creativity with us. This amazing book now allows us to return the favor.

Enjoy!
Draw!!
Listen to The Beach Boys!!!

- Howie Edelson, 2023

This **QR Code** will give you access to the official **Beach Boys Coloring Book** playlist!

The Beach Boys Surf's up Cafe Menu

Help me, Caesar!

Little Deuce Soup

The Warmth of the Bun
with Wild Honey

Surfer Spoon

Wouldn't it be Ice Cream
with California Swirls

Cocomo

Smiley Fries

Good Piebrations

Egg Sounds

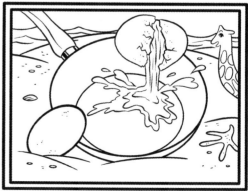

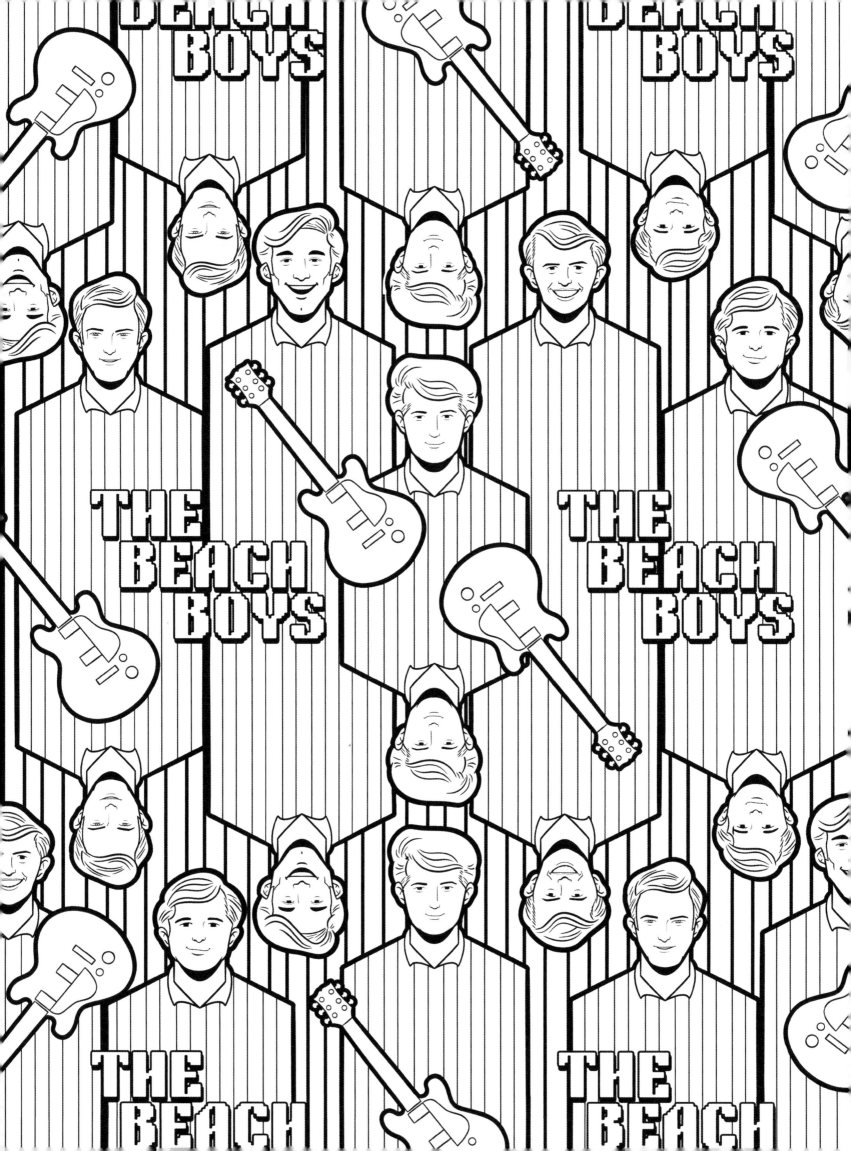

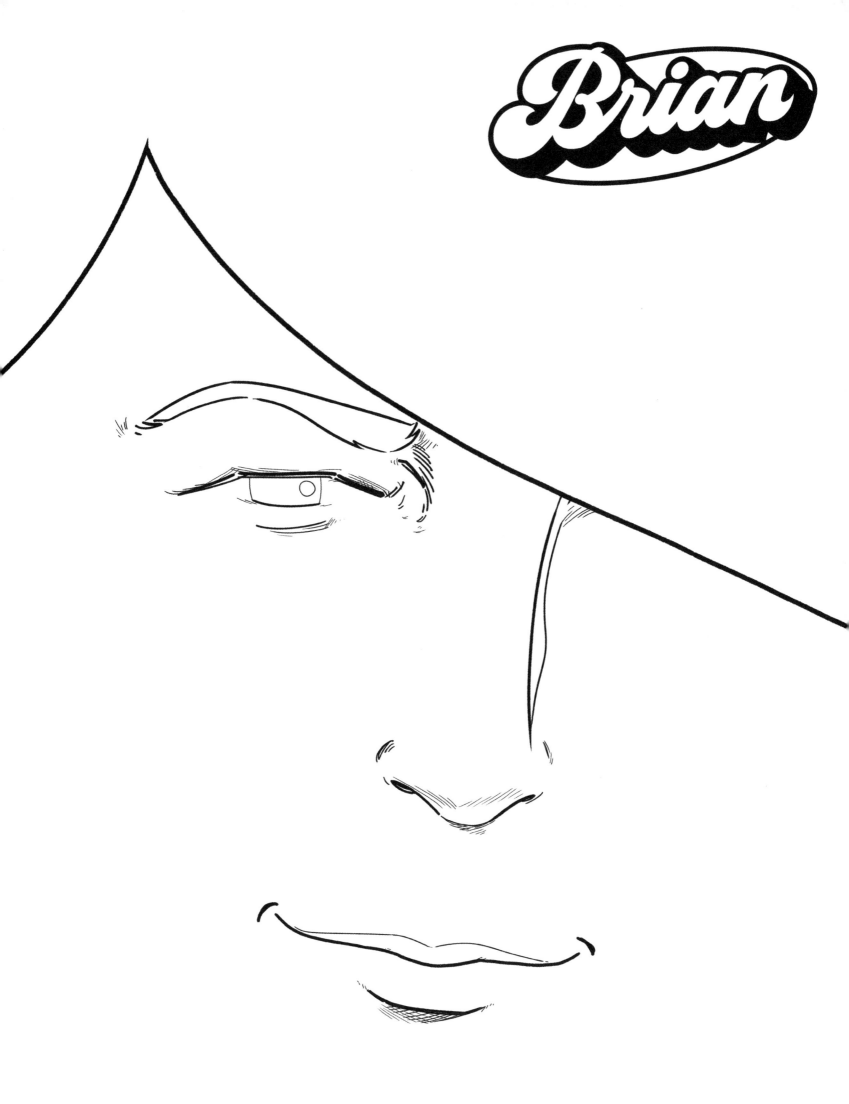

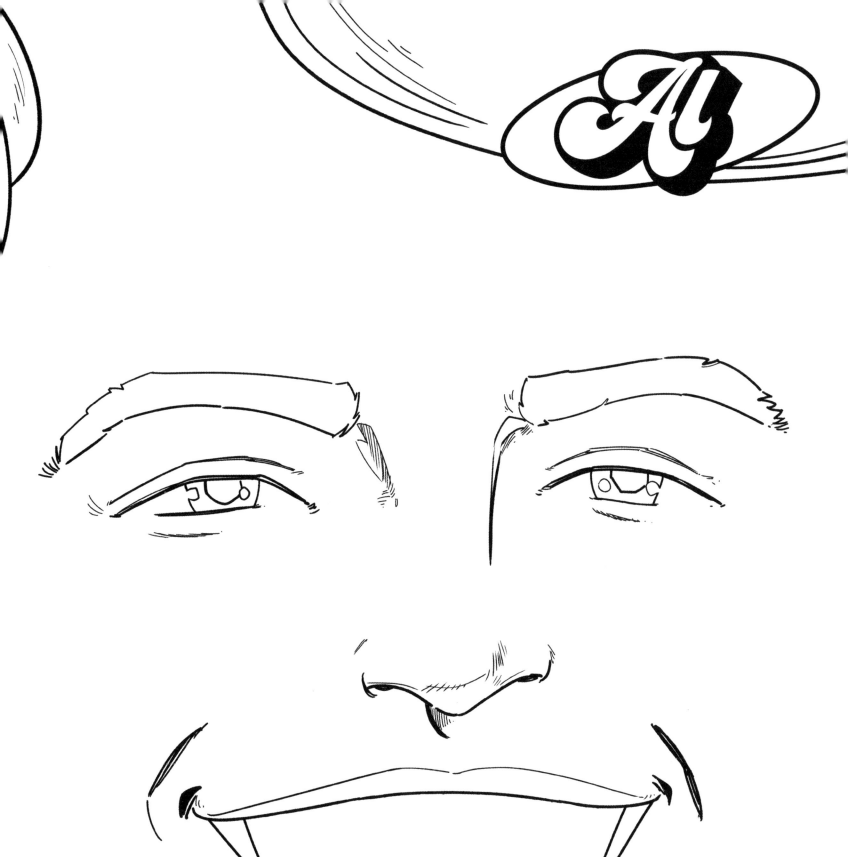

サーフィン◦サファリ

"Surfin' Safari" The Beach Boys

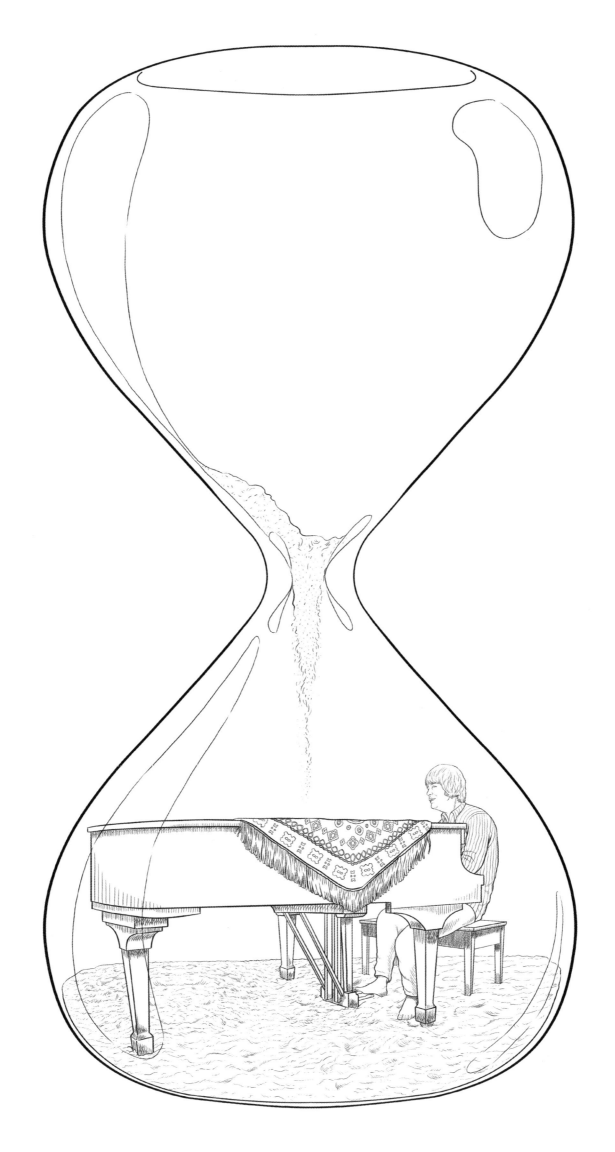

THE BEACH
BOYS

BROTHER PICTURES PRESENTS A *Beach Boys* FILM

CARO LINE

"A STORY FOR THE AGES!"
Steady Stone

"IT WILL BREAK YOUR HEART."
JARDINE POST

SOUNDTRACK AVAILABLE AT ALL THE BEST RECORD STORES!

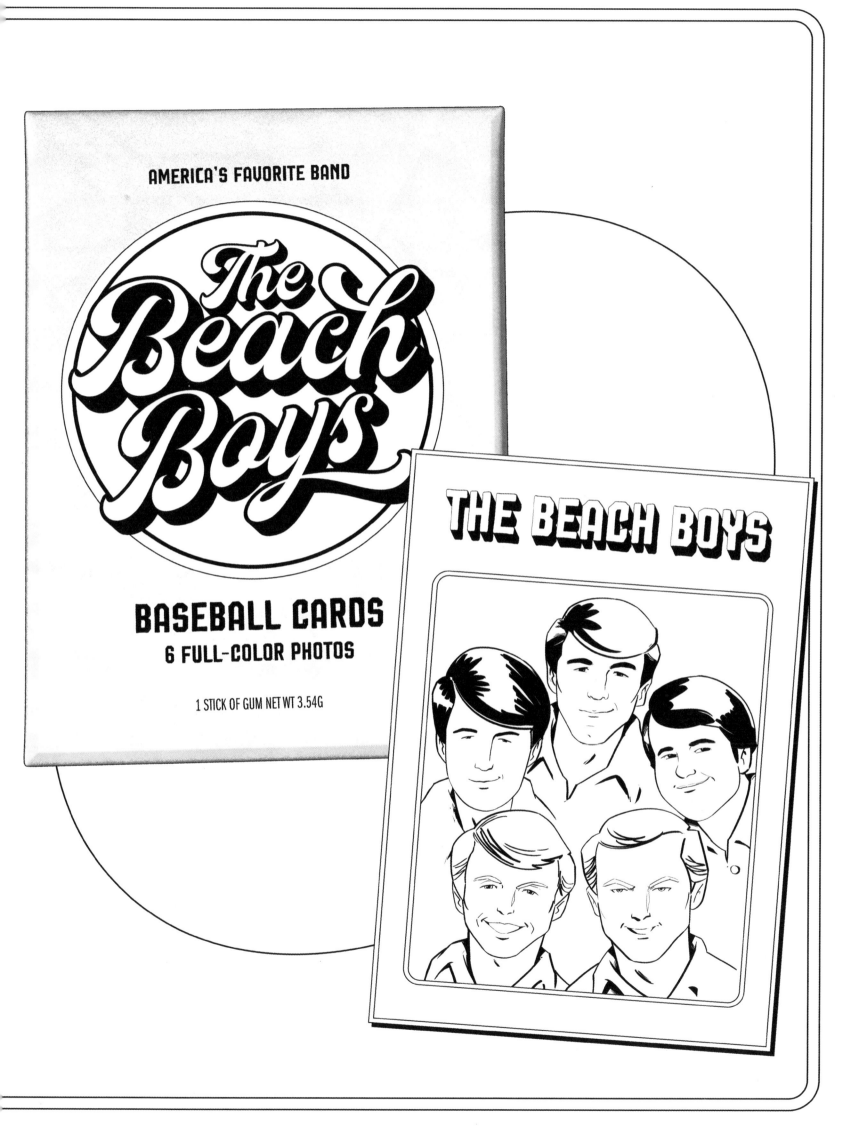

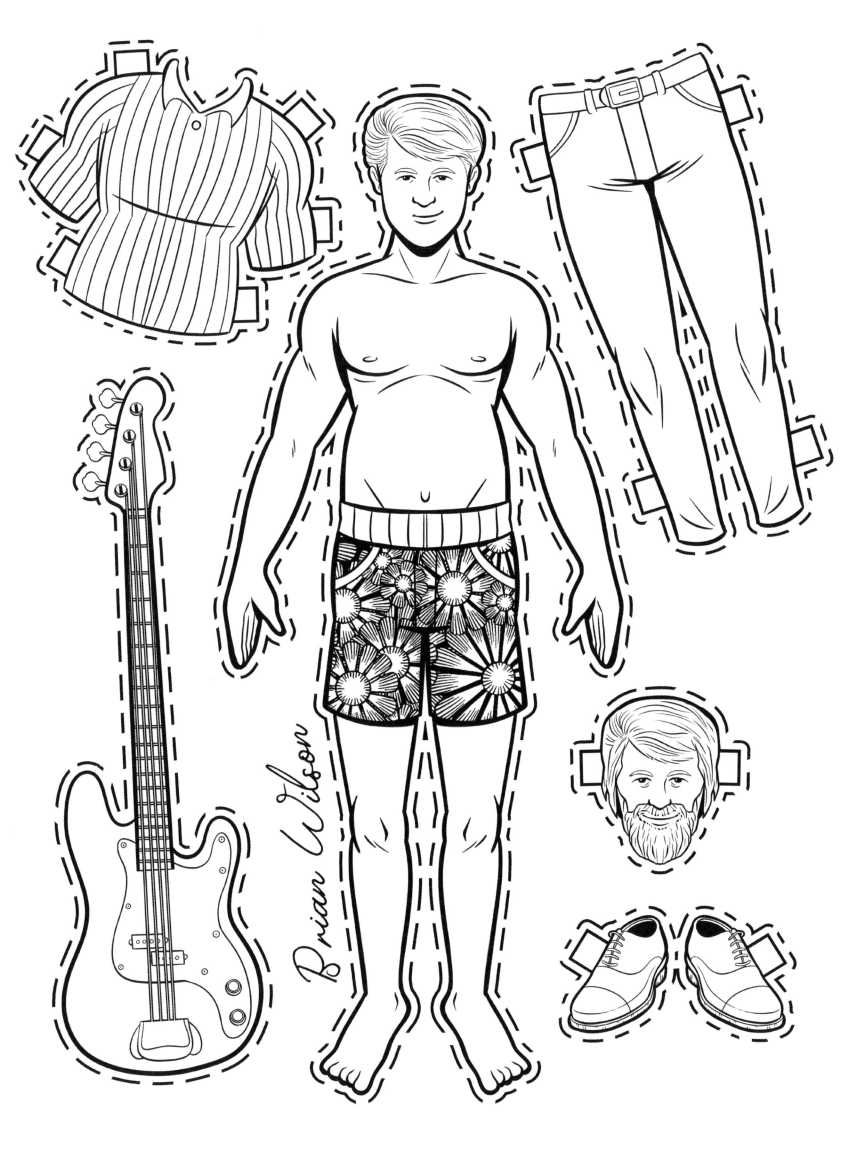

Brian Wilson

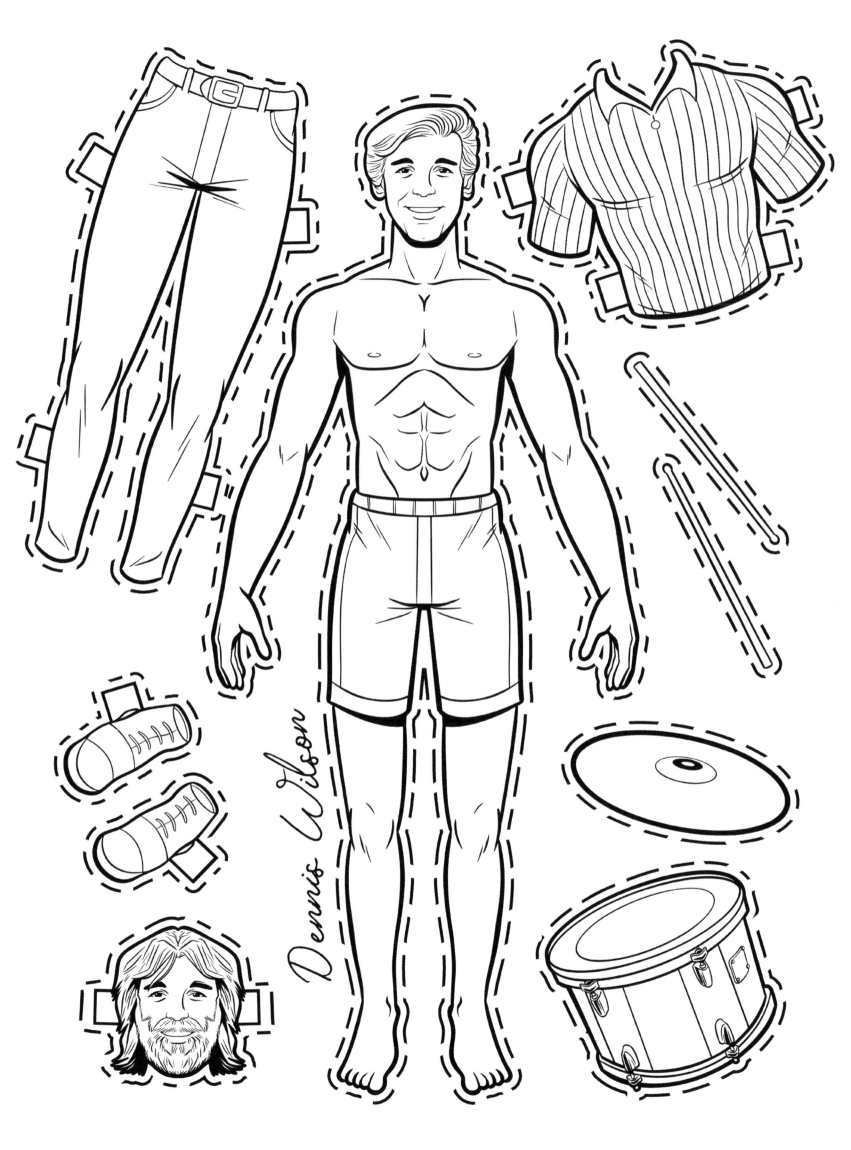

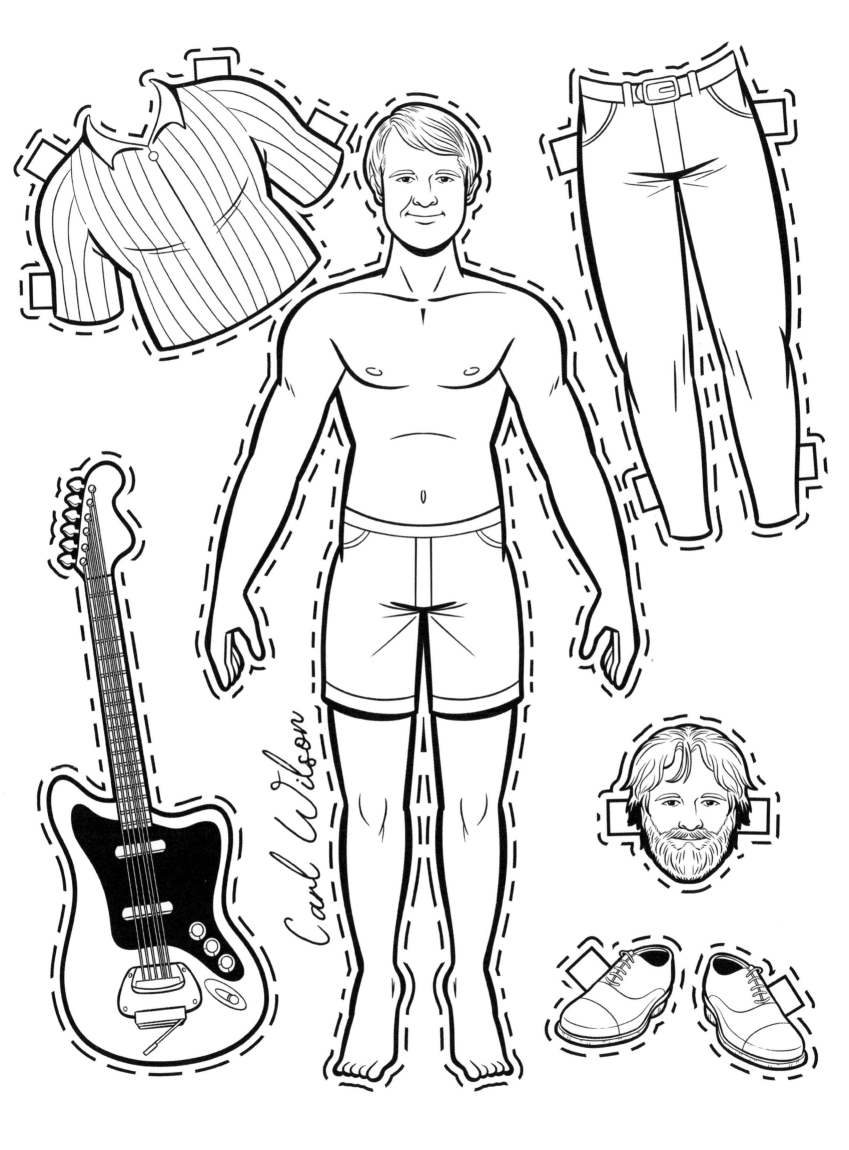

Carl Wilson

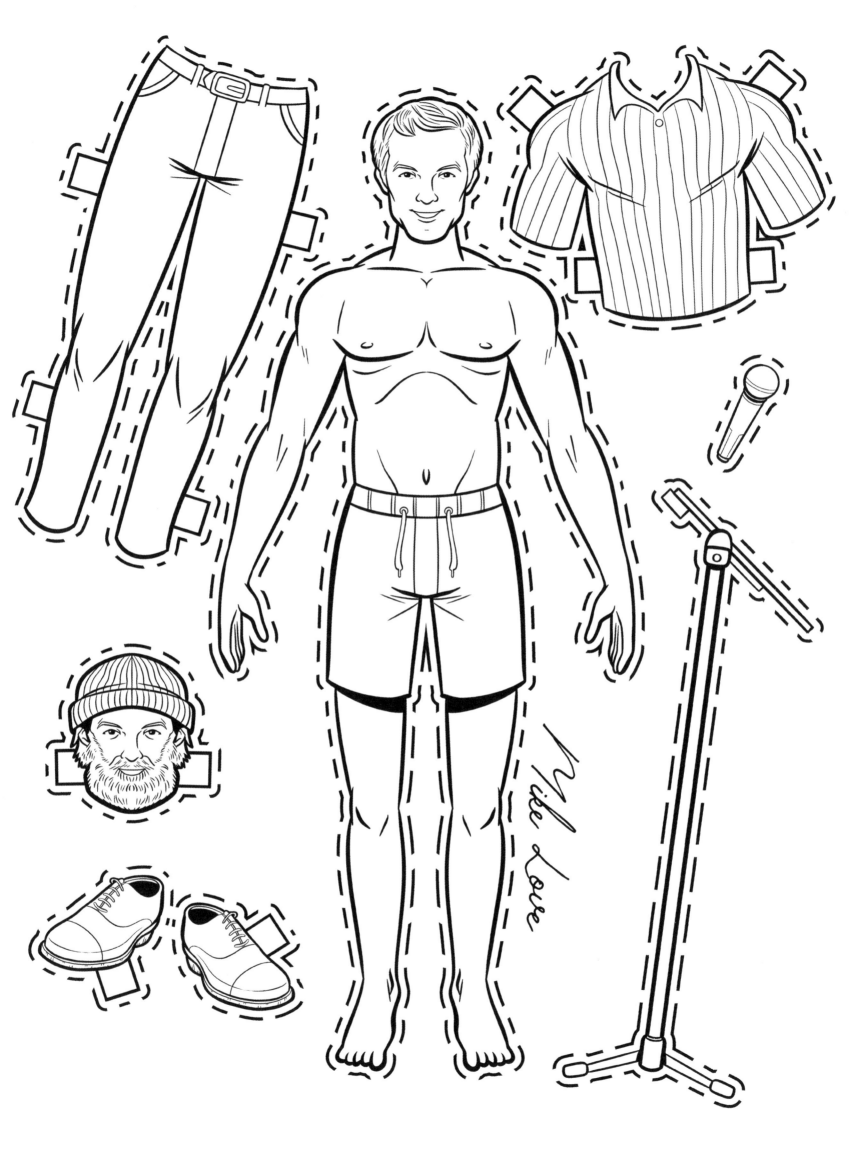

Mike Love

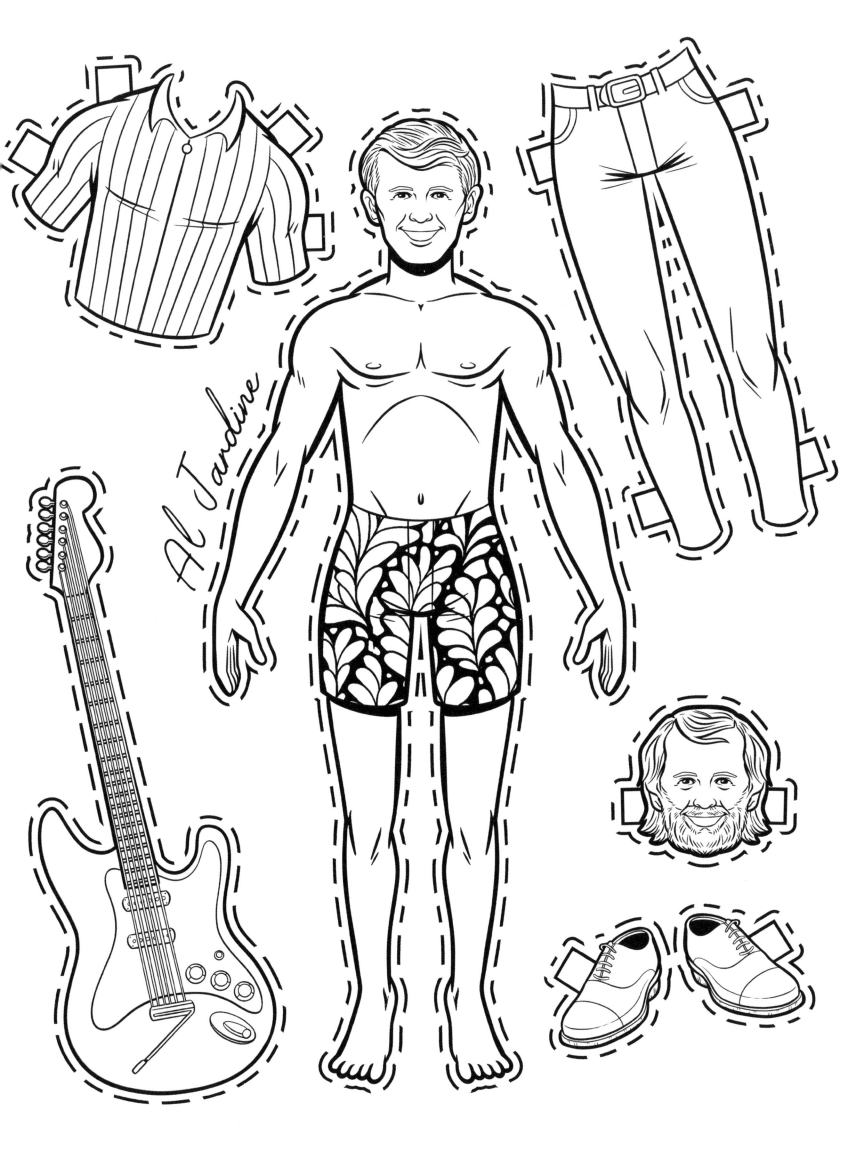

Al Jardine

THE BEACH BOYS: OFFICIAL COLORING BOOK

Created at Fantoons Animation Studios.

ART DIRECTION BY: David Calcano.

WRITTEN BY: David Calcano, Giggens, Juan Riera
and Lindsay Lee.

ILLUSTRATED BY: Juan Riera, Lindsay Lee, Jorge Mansilla,
Alberto Belandria and Larissa Rivero.

LETTERING BY: Eduardo Braun.

EDITED BY: Steve Colle.

PRODUCED BY: Linda Otero, Mariafernanda Fuentes and Diana Villena.

BOOK LAYOUT DESIGN BY: Brett Burner.

SPECIAL THANKS:

It is an absolute blast to be able to create this official Beach Boys book for
fellow fans and newcomers. The Beach Boys are musical geniuses that have
given us some of the greatest songs ever written in over 60 years of good
vibrations. We first shared our love for this astonishing band with the official
animated music video for "Little Saint Nick." Now, we are incredibly fortunate
to keep doing it with this book! How awesome is that?! I hope you enjoy these
pages as much as we did making them because you know what? We'd LOVE
to make more! Everyone on our team of writers, producers and artists
enjoyed every second of the art you'll see here. So put on a Beach Boys album
or playlist, turn the volume up and pick up your colors. Enjoy those
harmonies that keep painting our ears with joy every day.

David Calcano (Co-Founder, Fantoons Animation Studios)

FANTOONS

THE BEACH BOYS: OFFICIAL COLORING BOOK

Sales: info@fantoons.tv
fantoons.tv/books/
https://thebeachboys.com/

All Character Designs © 2023 Fantoons and Iconic Brothers IP LLC. The Beach Boys: The Official Coloring Book is produced by Fantoons, Woodland Hills, CA fantoons.tv/books/
© 2023 Iconic Brothers IP LLC. The Beach Boys ™ Under License to Iconic Brothers IP LLC.

Printed in China

Regular Edition ISBN: 978-1-970047-24-0